SUCCESSFUL S

JOURNAL

The Reader's Digest Association, Inc.
Pleasantville, New York/Montreal

A READER'S DIGEST BOOK

Editor: Carolyn T. Chubet
Designer: Elizabeth Tunnicliffe
Writer-Consultant: Thomas Christopher

Cover and interior illustrations:
Winter, spring, and fall: TCL/Masterfile.
Summer: Ron Rovtar/Photonica.

TABLE OF CONTENTS

■

■

We must cultivate our garden.
— Voltaire, *Candide*

HOW TO USE YOUR GARDENING JOURNAL

Seasoned gardeners know that some of their most important work is done not with a spade but with a pencil and a journal like this one. For good recordkeeping is at the heart of successful gardening—your notes enable you to build on past triumphs and to avoid repeating mistakes. This handy notebook will help you to plan beautiful and satisfying garden beds, and to care for and keep track of your garden plants as well. It will prove to be a personal gardening reference that will be useful for years to come.

The SUCCESSFUL GARDENING JOURNAL begins with a section on garden design, providing you with a checklist of design questions to ask yourself and space for you to write your answers. (Note, too, that sheets of graph paper are included here and at the back of the journal to aid planning.)
Next come the four seasonal sections—winter, spring, summer, and fall—each introduced by inspirational poetry and quotes along with some timely lists and hints. Each section has weekly fill-in pages that prompt you to record essential facts, such as weather, soil condition, plants in bloom, lawn, trees and shrubs,

 and more. The busiest gardening seasons, spring and fall, have extra pages for notes. If you spend a little time each week writing in these sections, you'll have a personal record of events and gardening tasks to guide you the next year. And since successful gardening is in large part a matter of timing, these seasonal pages also provide a running checklist of reminders of what gardeners are likely to be doing in various climates—cold, temperate, warm, and hot.

Following the seasonal pages is a special section of plant and vegetable profiles, offering a place to keep more detailed pedigree and performance notes on individual plants or crops. And when you are seeking plants or tools to complete any garden project, refer to the catalog directory. There you'll find some helpful resources—and a place to record your own discoveries.

To make your journal even more useful, a section called Helpful Information covers such essential topics as working with the soil, starting seeds, buying flowering plants, annuals, perennials, bulbs, buying trees and shrubs, pruning, and vegetables. Before you undertake a task in the  garden—or go shopping for plants—be sure to consult these handy pages. If you take a moment to browse through the journal, you will see how easy it is to put it to work and turn it into a personal handbook. Happy gardening!

PLANNING

I know a little garden close,

Set thick with lily and red rose,

Where I would wander if I might

From dewy morn to dewy night.

—William Morris,
The Life and Death of Jason, A Garden by the Sea

Planning a Garden

Each site is unique and every gardener has his or her own style and taste, thus no two gardens are ever exactly alike. But in every case, certain practical considerations must be addressed. To help you sort out these issues, this section provides a Designer's Checklist with space to fill in your answers, some tips on garden design, and two pages of graph paper so you can draw a plan of your garden (see below). More graph paper can be found at the back of the journal if you wish to work on more than one area of your yard.

Preparing and Using a Base Plan

The first step in creating a plan for your garden is to draw a base plan on the graph paper. Begin by sketching the outline of the area under review, adding all of the key existing elements such as trees and paths. Then draw an arrow to indicate which direction is north and mark the areas of sun and shade. If the area is large, each square of graph paper should probably represent one square foot; for smaller gardens you may wish to allow more than one square per foot. Once you have finished the base plan, use tracing paper overlays to try out several planting plans. You will likely run through several drafts before developing a planting scheme that suits you. Once you've finalized the design, transfer it to the base plan. The result will be a permanent—and useful—record of your garden's design.

This design process is valuable because it can reveal flaws—clashing colors, for example—that are easy to fix on paper, but expensive to correct in the field. In addition, you can count the squares and figure out how many square feet there are in the area. This will help you order plants and mulch in the right quantities.

TIPS FOR GARDEN DESIGN

Repeating shapes adds structure to the garden. In a long border plant groups of mounding shrubs at regular intervals to create smaller sections visually while tying the entire design together.

Vary plant types. To give a sense of texture and variety to a garden, plant deciduous and coniferous shrubs together, for example, with a ground cover and some flowers.

Keep winter in mind. You may wish to include a shrub that has interesting branches when leafless, such as the red-twigged dogwood (*Cornus alba* 'Sibirica'), to give a garden bed some visual interest in winter.

Choose plants that contrast with their backdrop. A white or pink geranium stands out against a red brick wall, and a purple- or magenta-flowered petunia makes a dramatic statement against a white surface. On dark surfaces, peach-colored daylily blossoms and silver artemisia foliage catch the eye.

Hot colors—bright reds, oranges, and yellows—leap out at the eye and have the effect of making large spaces seem smaller and more intimate.

Cool colors—purples, silvers, and blues—tend to recede into the background and can provide an illusion of greater space in a small or constricted area.

In shaded areas dark colors tend to get lost. To brighten up this type of garden, plant light-colored flowers, blossoms in shades of white, light pink, or pale blues or greens.

Designer's Checklist

Even before beginning the plan, it is wise to focus your vision of what you want to create by asking yourself the following questions:

What are the assets of the site? Are there plants, views, or other features I want to preserve, or even emphasize? *(Mark these on the plan first.)*

_____

_____

_____

What are the site's liabilities? Does it sit next to a noisy highway or overlook an unsightly view? Should I plan fences or add a screen?

_____

_____

_____

What is the character of the soil? (*The Cooperative Extension Service office in your county is a source of inexpensive and reliable tests. It's easier to select plantings that prefer your soil type than to doctor the soil to suit the plants.*)

_____

_____

_____

DESIGNER'S CHECKLIST *(Continued)*

What sort of vegetation is native to your site? *(A local nature center can usually provide an answer, and this knowledge can provide clues to successful planting.)*

_____

_____

_____

_____

What are the microclimates—areas where the topography (say, a north-facing slope) or a feature (perhaps a sheltering wall) modifies the local climate?

_____

_____

_____

Who will be using the garden? Should it be childproof? Accessible to seniors?

_____

_____

What are the seasons of greatest use? (*In Southern gardens that are too hot for summertime use, winter flowers may have the greatest impact; in Northern gardens, fragrant blossoms are especially welcome on summer evenings.*)

_____

_____

_____

Is there an accessible water source? (*If not, plan only drought-tolerant planting.*)

_____

How much sun falls on the site? What time of day does sun strike the garden? (*The degree of sun or shade must determine the character of the planting. Morning sun is not as likely to burn sensitive plans as the afternoon sun is.*)

_____

_____

_____

How much maintenance are you willing to undertake? (*Flowers are pretty, but not when neglected. A busy gardener should consider informal designs that require less upkeep, and substitute ground covers for lawns and flower beds.*)

_____

_____

_____

WINTER

Sometimes hath the brightest day a cloud;

And after summer evermore succeeds

Barren winter, with his wrathful nipping cold:

So cares and joys abound, as seasons fleet.

—William Shakespeare, *King Henry VI*

*I have often wondered that those who…
love to live in gardens, have never
thought of contriving a Winter Garden,
which should consist of such trees only as
never cast their leaves.…I have so far
indulged myself in this thought, that I
have set apart a whole acre of ground for
the executing of it. The walls are covered
with ivy.…The laurel, the hornbeam,
and the holly, with many other trees and
plants…grow so thick in it, that you
cannot imagine a more lively scene.*

—Joseph Addison, *The Spectator*

FOR YOU THERE'S
ROSEMARY AND RUE;
THESE KEEP
SEEMING AND SAVOR ALL
THE WINTER LONG.

—William Shakespeare,
The Winter's Tale

Special Protection in Winter

To protect tender Southern plants when nighttime temperatures dip a few degrees below 32°F (0°C), turn on the sprinkler. The water droplets chill more slowly than the surrounding air and can fend off a mild frost.

Keeping Plants Cool

Thawing on sunny days followed by refreezing may damage plants that are otherwise hardy. A blanket of evergreen boughs or a mulch of straw keeps perennials evenly cold; a shield of burlap helps protect shrubs.

When the Winter Wind Blows

Cold winter winds dehydrate evergreens, which lose moisture through their needles or leaves. And when the ground is frozen, plants cannot absorb water to replace the moisture they have lost. Spray evergreens with antidesiccants, and water deeply during thaws.

ANNUALS

—— for winter bloom in mild-winter regions ——

AFRICAN DAISY *(Dimorphotheca sinuata)*
yellow, orange, red, white flowers

CORNFLOWER *(Centaurea cyanus)*
blue, purple, pink, white flowers

FLOWERING CABBAGE, FLOWERING KALE
(Brassica oleracea)
purple, pink, white flowers

GODETIA *(Clarkia amoena)*
crimson, pink, white flowers

LARKSPUR *(Consolida ambigua)*
white, blue, pink, red flowers

NEMESIA *(Nemesia strumosa)*
white, yellow, pink, orange, purple flowers

PANSY *(Viola x wittrockiana)*
purple, maroon, red, yellow, orange, white flowers

POOR MAN'S ORCHID *(Schizanthus pinnatus)*
purple, white, red, pink flowers

POT MARIGOLD *(Calendula officinalis)*
yellow, orange, cream flowers

SNAPDRAGONS *(Antirrhinum majus)*
red, white, yellow, orange, pink, purplish flowers

Trees & Shrubs
—— *with vivid bark for winter color* ——

Yellow

Golden willow *(Salix alba vitellina)*

Yellowtwig dogwood *(Cornus stolonifera flaviramea)*

Red

Dwarf European cranberry *(Viburnum opulus nanum)*

Red osier dogwood *(Cornus stolonifera)*

Red-stem willow *(Salix alba* 'Chermesina'*)*

Scotch pine *(Pinus sylvestris)*

Siberian dogwood *(Cornus alba* 'Sibirica'*)*

Sweetbells *(Leucothoe racemosa)*

Wingthorn rose *(Rosa sericea pteracantha)*

White

Canoe birch *(Betula papyrifera)*

Quaking aspen *(Populus tremuloides)*

Green

Kerria *(Kerria japonica)*

Striped maple *(Acer pennsylvanicum)*

Broom *(Cytisus)*

NORTHERN SHRUBS
—— that bloom during winter thaws ——

FRAGRANT WINTER HAZEL (*Corylopsis glabrescens*)
yellow flowers, fragrant

CHINESE WITCH HAZEL (*Hamamelis mollis*)
yellow, red flowers, fragrant

WINTER SWEET (*Chimonanthus praecox*)
yellow-striped purplish brown flowers, fragrant

WINTER JASMINE (*Jasminum nudiflorum*)
yellow flowers, no fragrance

WINTER HONEYSUCKLE (*Lonicera fragrantissima*)
creamy white flowers, intensely fragrant

DECEMBER

Weather _____

Soil Conditions _____

In Bloom _____

_____

Flower Garden _____

Trees & Shrubs _____

Lawn _____

Fruits & Vegetables _____

_____

Notes _____

_____

C H E C K L I S T

COLD

❏ Brush heavy snow off evergreens branches to prevent breakage.

❏ Protect the bark of young trees from nibbling rodents by encircling trunks with fine wire mesh.

TEMPERATE

❏ Drain fuel from lawn mower, sharpen the blade, and store in a secure, dry place.

❏ Put plastic bags filled with insulating straw or leaves around cold-sensitive herbs such as rosemary.

Weather _____

Soil Conditions _____

In Bloom _____

_____

Flower Garden _____

Trees & Shrubs _____

Lawn _____

Fruits & Vegetables _____

_____

Notes _____

_____

WARM

- ❏ Treat lawn with postemergent herbicides to control annual grass-es and broadleaf weeds and help next year's Bermuda grass.
- ❏ Fill beds with hardy annuals, such as pansies, for winter color.

HOT

- ❏ Transplant deciduous trees, such as cassias and orchid trees.
- ❏ Remove aging warm-weather annuals and replace with plantings of ornamental kale, cabbage, and other winter plants.

DECEMBER

Weather _____

Soil Conditions _____

In Bloom _____

_____

Flower Garden _____

Trees & Shrubs _____

Lawn _____

Fruits & Vegetables _____

_____

Notes _____

_____

C H E C K L I S T

COLD

- ❏ Clean, sharpen, and repair garden tools; wipe wooden handles with linseed oil.
- ❏ To prevent damage to nearby lawn, use cat litter or sand—not salt—to ensure traction on icy walks.

TEMPERATE

- ❏ If garden soil tests too acidic, add lime now so that beds will adjust by spring.
- ❏ Drain any irrigation systems before freezing weather sets in.

Weather _____

Soil Conditions _____

In Bloom _____

_____

Flower Garden _____

Trees & Shrubs _____

Lawn _____

Fruits & Vegetables _____

_____

Notes _____

_____

WARM

- ❏ Add a layer of mulch around trees and shrubs to protect them against drying winter winds.
- ❏ Protect tender plants against frost damage in upland and inland regions.

HOT

- ❏ Divide and replant overgrown perennials.
- ❏ Apply postemergent herbicides to lawn to reduce broadleaf weeds.
- ❏ Prune roses; cut the canes back by one-third to one-half.

JANUARY
WEEK 1

Weather _____

Soil Conditions _____

In Bloom _____

_____

Flower Garden _____

Trees & Shrubs _____

Lawn _____

Fruits & Vegetables _____

_____

Notes _____

_____

C H E C K L I S T

COLD

- ❑ Blanket beds with boughs of discarded Christmas trees to protect hardy perennials against sudden damaging thaws.

- ❑ Review expiration dates on pesticides and other garden chemicals; dispose of outdated materials.

TEMPERATE

- ❑ Leave any cold-damaged foliage on evergreen shrubs until spring.

- ❑ Order seeds and supplies.

Weather _____

Soil Conditions _____

In Bloom _____

_____

Flower Garden _____

Trees & Shrubs _____

Lawn _____

Fruits & Vegetables _____

_____

Notes _____

_____

WARM

- ❏ Prune crape myrtles, chaste trees, and pomegranates back to 1-in/2.5-cm-dia branches to encourage larger flowers in summer.
- ❏ Sow seeds of slow-growing annuals, such as wax begonias and gerberas, indoors.

HOT

- ❏ Wrap the growing points of young palms with foam rubber to protect from penetrating cold.
- ❏ Deadhead winter annuals to rejuvenate and prolong flowering.

JANUARY

Weather _____

Soil Conditions _____

In Bloom _____

_____

Flower Garden _____

Trees & Shrubs _____

Lawn _____

Fruits & Vegetables _____

_____

Notes _____

_____

C H E C K L I S T

COLD

- ❏ Save wood ashes (a good source of potassium) in a dry container to spread on garden beds in spring.

- ❏ Test germination rate of leftover vegetable seeds by spreading samples on a moist paper towel. If samples produce few sprouts, discard seed.

TEMPERATE

- ❏ Be prepared to protect tender early-flowering bulbs from sudden frosts and cold spells.

- ❏ Water trees, shrubs, and roses deeply during thaws.

Weather _____

Soil Conditions _____

In Bloom _____

_____

Flower Garden _____

Trees & Shrubs _____

Lawn _____

Fruits & Vegetables _____

_____

Notes _____

_____

WARM

❑ Set out cool-season vegetable and herb transplants; direct-seed parsley, cilantro, thyme, and chives.

❑ Start tomato, pepper, and eggplant seeds indoors; plant peas, carrots, beets, and radishes directly into the garden.

HOT

❑ Fertilize lawn now if turf is green; aerate turf to enhance water absorption.

❑ Start tomato, pepper, and eggplant seeds indoors; plant peas, carrots, beets, and radishes directly into the garden.

FEBRUARY

Weather _____

Soil Conditions _____

In Bloom _____

_____

Flower Garden _____

Trees & Shrubs _____

Lawn _____

Fruits & Vegetables _____

_____

Notes _____

_____

C H E C K L I S T

COLD

- ❏ Water trees and shrubs—especially evergreens—during thaws.
- ❏ Prune fruit trees: apples, pears, cherries, etc.
- ❏ Place orders for seeds, shrubs, trees, and perennials with mail-order nurseries.

TEMPERATE

- ❏ Prune back overgrown yew or privet hedges, cut trunks to a point 1 ft/30 cm below the desired final height of the hedge.
- ❏ Sow seeds of slow-growing annuals, such as wax begonias and gerberas, indoors.

Weather _____

Soil Conditions _____

In Bloom _____

_____

Flower Garden _____

Trees & Shrubs _____

Lawn _____

Fruits & Vegetables _____

_____

Notes _____

_____

WARM

- ❏ Apply dormant oil to camellias and evergreen hollies to eradicate scale insects and kill overwintering insect eggs.

- ❏ Plant new roses; prune established rosebushes when emerging shoots are 1 in/2.5 cm long.

HOT

- ❏ Plant potatoes; begin planting of warm-weather crops, such as beans, corn, melons, and squash. Set out tomato, eggplant, and pepper seedlings.

- ❏ Sow marigolds and zinnias directly into the garden.

Weather _____

Soil Conditions _____

In Bloom _____

_____

Flower Garden _____

Trees & Shrubs _____

Lawn _____

Fruits & Vegetables _____

_____

Notes _____

_____

C H E C K L I S T

COLD

- ❏ Sow seeds of onions and leeks and cabbage family crops (broccoli, Brussels sprouts, etc.) indoors.

- ❏ Disinfect last year's seed-starting flats and pots. Soak them in a 1:10 solution of bleach and water.

TEMPERATE

- ❏ On sunny days ventilate roses over-wintering in plastic-foam rose cones.

- ❏ Shop at garden centers now—before the spring rush. The sales staff has time to advise on products and plants, and the shelves are likely to be well-stocked.

Weather _____

Soil Conditions _____

In Bloom _____

_____

Flower Garden _____

Trees & Shrubs _____

Lawn _____

Fruits & Vegetables _____

_____

Notes _____

_____

WARM

- ❏ Plant potatoes and warm-weather crops, such as beans, corn, melons, and squash. Set out tomato, eggplant, and pepper seedlings.

- ❏ Order new perennials and plant them as soon as they arrive. This is especially important for lily bulbs.

HOT

- ❏ Apply dormant oil to evergreens to kill scale insects and overwintering insect eggs; apply insecticidal soap as needed to control spider mites.

- ❏ Begin weekly spraying of roses with fungicide to protect foliage against black spot and powdery mildew.

SPRING

The thirsty earth soaks up the rain,

And drinks, and gapes for drink again.

The plants suck in the earth, and are

With constant drinking fresh and fair.

—Abraham Cowley, *Anacreon*

For winter's rains and ruins are over,

And all the season of snows and sins;

The days dividing lover and lover,

The light that loses, the night that wins;

And time remembered is grief forgotten,

And frosts are slain and flowers begotten,

And in green underwood and cover

Blossom by blossom the spring begins.

—Algernon Charles Swinburne
Atalanta in Calydon

BUT EACH SPRING...
A GARDENING INSTINCT,
SURE AS THE SAP RISING
IN THE TREES, STIRS
WITHIN US.

WE LOOK ABOUT AND
DECIDE TO TAME ANOTHER
LITTLE BIT OF GROUND.

—Lewis Gannett

Uncovering the Plants

Periodically check under the blankets of mulch or tree boughs applied the previous year as winter protection. Swelling buds or new shoots are signs that it's time to uncover the plants.

When to Prune Roses

Don't be too quick to prune back rose bushes—this may stimulate early growth that is vulnerable to late frosts. Don't prune until the new shoots are 1 in/2.5 cm long.

After the Bulbs Bloom

There is a temptation to snip off the leaves from perennial bulbs after they finish flowering, but this is when the plants are making and storing food for next year's bloom. Let bulb foliage yellow and wither naturally before removing it.

Tending to the Lawn

To control crabgass most effectively, apply a preemergent herbicide to the lawn when the forsythias bloom.

In the South the arrival of warmer temperatures means it's time to fertilize Bermuda grass and St. Augustine grass lawns. Early spring is the best time to sow grass seed or lay sod in areas that suffer from extreme summer heat combined with drought.

PLANTING SEEDLINGS

When planting out seedlings grown in peat pots, be sure to tear off the top 1/2 in/1.3 cm of each pot. If the pots protrude above the soil surface, they act as wicks to draw moisture up and away from the seedlings' roots.

To protect seedlings from an overnight frost, make hot caps out of empty milk jugs. Cut the bottoms from the jugs and set them down over the plants as the sun is setting. Be sure to remove the jugs the next morning before sunlight turns them into solar collectors and overheats the seedlings within.

Seedlings started indoors should be hardened off before they are transplanted into the garden. Two weeks before transplanting, begin setting the seedlings outdoors in a sunny, sheltered spot. Leave them outside for about 30 minutes the first day, and gradually increase the interval until the seedlings are spending several hours outdoors each day. This will reduce transplant shock.

PLAN LONG-LASTING HARVESTS

Plant spring greens bit by bit. Sowing several rows of lettuce, spinach, or arugula all at once yields a flood of produce—too much of each crop will mature at the same time. Instead, sow half a row of mixed greens every week until midspring. The result will be a long-lasting harvest. (This method also works for corn and beans.)

Planting Partners
to accompany spring bulbs

Bugle (*Ajuga reptans* 'Multicoloris')
ground cover with bronze-pink-and-yellow foliage

Leopard's bane (*Doronicum cordatum* 'Madame Mason')
perennial with bright yellow flowers

Wallflower (*Erysimum cheiri*)
perennial with orange, red, white, purple flowers

Dead nettle (*Lamium maculatum*)
ground cover with silver-variegated foliage

Honesty (*Lunaria rediviva*)
perennial with pale purple flowers

Virginia bluebells (*Mertensia virginica*)
perennial with blue, pink, white flowers

Forget-me-nots (*Myosotis sylvatica & M.* 'Royal Blue')
annual with blue, pink, white flowers

Korean rhododendron (*Rhododendron mucronulatum*)
shrub with rose-purple flowers on bare branches

Japanese spirea (*Spiraea japonica* 'Goldflame')
dwarf shrub with orange-red new foliage

Pansy (*Viola* x *wittockiana*)
annual with purple, blue, red, orange, yellow, white flowers

SPRING-FLOWERING TREES

—— 10 in order of bloom ——

CORNELIAN CHERRY (*Cornus mas*)
yellow flowers

SPRING CHERRY (*Prunus subhirtella*)
pink flowers

STAR MAGNOLIA (*Magnolia stellata*)
white, fragrant flowers

EASTERN REDBUD (*Cercis canadensis*)
purplish pink flowers

JAPANESE FLOWERING CHERRY (*Prunus serrulata*)
white to pink flowers

SAUCER MAGNOLIA (*Magnolia* x *soulangiana*)
white to purple flowers

JAPANESE CRAB APPLE (*Malus floribunda*)
deep pink to white flowers

CAROLINA SILVERBELL (*Halesia carolina*)
white flowers

GOLDEN CHAIN (*Laburnum wateri* 'Vossii')
yellow flowers

Weather _____

Soil Conditions _____

In Bloom _____

_____

Flower Garden _____

Trees & Shrubs _____

Lawn _____

Fruits & Vegetables _____

_____

Notes _____

_____

C H E C K L I S T

COLD

- ❏ During mild days spray trees, shrubs, and roses with dormant oil to kill overwintering insect pests and their eggs.

- ❏ To promote growth and provide material for cuttings, fertilize pots of annuals—coleuses, geraniums, and impatiens—overwintered indoors.

TEMPERATE

- ❏ Prune back forsythias, spiraeas, and other early-blooming shrubs when flowers fade.

- ❏ Fertilize trees and shrubs as growth starts.

- ❏ Remove winter mulch from perennial beds.

Weather _____

Soil Conditions _____

In Bloom _____

_____

Flower Garden _____

Trees & Shrubs _____

Lawn _____

Fruits & Vegetables _____

_____

Notes _____

_____

WARM

❑ Apply preemergent herbicide around perennials and shrubs to prevent spring-germinating weeds.

❑ Fertilize camellias after flowering; fertilize other shrubs and trees after their growth starts.

HOT

❑ Apply foliar fertilizer to emerging foliage of palms damaged by unusually cold weather.

❑ Prune young azaleas after bloom to encourage compact growth.

❑ Fill beds with plantings of heat-loving annuals.

Weather _____

Soil Conditions _____

In Bloom _____

_____

Flower Garden _____

Trees & Shrubs _____

Lawn _____

Fruits & Vegetables _____

_____

Notes _____

_____

C H E C K L I S T

COLD

- ❑ Apply high-phosphate fertilizer to bulb plantings.
- ❑ On sunny days ventilate roses overwintered in plastic-foam cones.
- ❑ Sow seeds indoors for peppers, eggplant, early tomatoes, and other warm-weather crops.

TEMPERATE

- ❑ Plant out cold-tolerant annuals, such as pansies and stocks.
- ❑ Remove winter protection from rosebushes as the leaf buds swell and open.

Weather _____

Soil Conditions _____

In Bloom _____

_____

Flower Garden _____

Trees & Shrubs _____

Lawn _____

Fruits & Vegetables _____

_____

Notes _____

_____

WARM

- ❏ Plant out summer-flowering annuals.
- ❏ Deadhead spring-flowering bulbs, but avoid removing foliage until it yellows and dries.
- ❏ Begin weekly sprays to protect roses from black spot and mildew.

HOT

- ❏ Plant lilies and tuberous begonias for summer bloom.
- ❏ Fertilize lawn; mow more often as growth increases.
- ❏ Apply preemergent herbicide to lawn to control annual weeds.

C H E C K L I S T

COLD

❏ Start seeds of slower-growing annuals, such as wax begonias and gerberas, indoors.

❏ Rake and mow lawn; aerate to improve water, fertilizer, and air penetration to grass roots.

TEMPERATE

❏ Sow pepper, eggplant, and tomato seeds indoors.

❏ Sow cold-tolerant crops, such as spinach and peas, into garden beds.

❏ Rake and mow lawn; aerate to improve water, fertilizer, and air penetration to grass roots.

WARM

- ❏ Prune everblooming roses; spray rosebushes with dormant oil to control scale, aphids, whiteflies, and spider mites.

- ❏ Plant warm-weather crops, such as beans, corn, cucumbers, melons, squashes, okra, and sweet potatoes.

HOT

- ❏ Water roses deeply during dry weather; apply slow-release fertilizer to established bushes.

- ❏ Foliar-feed vegetable plants with soluble fertilizer; mulch to protect from drought.

Weather _____

Soil Conditions _____

In Bloom _____

_____

Flower Garden _____

Trees & Shrubs _____

Lawn _____

Fruits & Vegetables _____

_____

Notes _____

_____

C H E C K L I S T

COLD

- ❏ Fertilize deciduous shrubs and trees, and hollies.

- ❏ Cut back forsythia, spiraea, and other early-blooming shrubs after flowers fade.

- ❏ Remove winter mulch from perennial, herb and bulb beds as plants sprout.

TEMPERATE

- ❏ To encourage compact growth, prune young azaleas, wisterias, and jasmines after blooming.

- ❏ Start seeds of fast-growing annuals, such as marigolds and zinnias, indoors.

Weather _____

Soil Conditions _____

In Bloom _____

_____

Flower Garden _____

Trees & Shrubs _____

Lawn _____

Fruits & Vegetables _____

_____

Notes _____

_____

WARM

❏ To promote compact growth, prune azaleas, wisterias, and jasmines after flowering; prune hollies and nandinas now.

❏ Plant summer bulbs: begonia, canna, crinum, dahlia, agapanthus, montbretia, and gladiolus.

HOT

❏ Transplant palms now.

❏ Spray lightweight summer oil on citrus to control scale insects.

❏ As winter plantings of annuals are removed, renew beds with organic matter, lime, and fertilizer.

Weather _____

Soil Conditions _____

In Bloom _____

_____

Flower Garden _____

Trees & Shrubs _____

Lawn _____

Fruits & Vegetables _____

_____

Notes _____

_____

C H E C K L I S T

COLD

- ❏ Remove winter protection from roses as leaf buds swell and open, and apply a slow-release fertilizer.

- ❏ Start seeds of fast-growing annuals—marigolds and nicotianas—indoors.

- ❏ Apply slow-release 3-1-2 fertilizer to lawn at recommended rate.

TEMPERATE

- ❏ After spring-flowering bulbs bloom, leave foliage intact until it yellows and dries.

- ❏ Prune everblooming rosebushes. Lightly prune climbing ever-blooming types but leave the main canes alone.

Weather _____

Soil Conditions _____

In Bloom _____

_____

Flower Garden _____

Trees & Shrubs _____

Lawn _____

Fruits & Vegetables _____

_____

Notes _____

_____

WARM

- ❑ Deadhead perennials and cut back hard after flowering to promote plant vigor and rebloom.
- ❑ Watch roses for powdery mildew; continue weekly sprays with fungicide.

HOT

- ❑ Deadhead perennials and cut back after bloom to promote plant vigor and rebloom.
- ❑ Side-dress heavy feeders, such as corn, peppers, and tomatoes, with a complete fertilizer.

C H E C K L I S T

COLD

❏ Spade or till vegetable and flower beds as soon as soil dries sufficiently (when it does not make a tight, wet ball when squeezed).

❏ Plant seed potatoes in the garden. Transplant into the garden the seedlings of the cabbage family: cabbage, broccoli, and kohlrabi.

TEMPERATE

❏ Divide and replant overgrown perennials.

❏ Plant out seedlings of cabbage family. Sow peas, lettuce, spinach, radishes, beets, and carrots.

❏ Apply slow-release 3-1-2 fertilizer to lawn at recommended rate.

_____

_____

_____

_____

_____

_____

_____

_____

_____

WARM

- ❏ Side-dress heavy feeders, such as corn, peppers, and tomatoes, with complete fertilizer.
- ❏ Continue planting hot-weather crops, such as okra and black-eyed peas.
- ❏ Begin sodding with Bermuda grass anytime now through October.

HOT

- ❏ Water roses deeply in dry weather and apply a slow-release fertilizer.
- ❏ Continue planting hot-weather crops, such as okra, black-eyed peas, bush beans, and corn.
- ❏ Plant sod or sprigs of St. Augustine, centipede, and Bermuda grasses.

Weather _____

Soil Conditions _____

In Bloom _____

_____

Flower Garden _____

Trees & Shrubs _____

Lawn _____

Fruits & Vegetables _____

_____

Notes _____

_____

C H E C K L I S T

COLD

- ❑ Spread a 1–2-in/2.5–5-cm-thick blanket of organic mulch around shrubs and at the bases of trees.

- ❑ Snap off the top half of "candles," or new growth, of pines, firs, and other conifers to encourage compact growth.

TEMPERATE

- ❑ Plant out remaining annual seedlings after all danger of frost has passed.

- ❑ Apply summer mulch around established plantings of annuals and perennials.

Weather _____

Soil Conditions _____

In Bloom _____

_____

Flower Garden _____

Trees & Shrubs _____

Lawn _____

Fruits & Vegetables _____

_____

Notes _____

_____

WARM

- ❏ Apply granular fertilizer to crape myrtles and other flowering shrubs to encourage better bloom.
- ❏ Spray trees and shrubs with insecticidal soap to control whiteflies and aphids that cause sooty mold.

HOT

- ❏ Spray insecticidal soap to control spider mites on crotons, azaleas, and camphor trees.
- ❏ Water new shrubs and trees and roses weekly in dry weather.
- ❏ Dethatch Bermuda grass lawns.

Weather _____

Soil Conditions _____

In Bloom _____

_____

Flower Garden _____

Trees & Shrubs _____

Lawn _____

Fruits & Vegetables _____

_____

Notes _____

_____

C H E C K L I S T

COLD

- ❏ As soon as danger of frost is past, set out flower and vegetable seedlings in the garden.

- ❏ Plant up outdoor tubs, window boxes, and other containers, but be prepared to move plants indoors if late frost threatens.

TEMPERATE

- ❏ Deadhead perennials and cut them back after flowering, to promote plant vigor and rebloom.

- ❏ Apply a complete granular fertilizer to roses. Watch for aphids, and spray the bushes with insecticidal soap as needed.

Weather _____

Soil Conditions _____

In Bloom _____

_____

Flower Garden _____

Trees & Shrubs _____

Lawn _____

Fruits & Vegetables _____

_____

Notes _____

_____

WARM

❏ As winter plantings of annuals are replaced, renew beds with organic matter, fertilizer, and lime (if needed).

❏ Sow fast-growing, warm-weather annuals, such as zinnias and marigolds, directly into garden.

HOT

❏ Apply summer mulch around annual and perennial plantings to protect from drought.

❏ Continue deadheading annuals and perennials; cut back perennials after they bloom.

C H E C K L I S T

COLD

- ❏ Begin weekly spraying of roses with fungicide to protect foliage from mildew and black spot.

- ❏ Prune everblooming roses (such as floribundas and hybrid teas) when their new shoots are 1 in/2.5 cm long.

TEMPERATE

- ❏ Plant out seedlings of cucumbers, melons, peppers, and tomatoes.

- ❏ Sow corn, beans, and pumpkins.

- ❏ Mow lawn regularly.

- ❏ Plant zoysia lawns by sodding, plugging, or sprigging.

WARM

- ☐ Spread summer mulch around perennials and roses to protect them from drought.

- ☐ Make last plantings of hot-weather vegetables, such as okra, black-eyed peas, and sweet potatoes.

- ☐ Dethatch Bermuda grass lawns.

HOT

- ☐ Watch roses for spider mites and spray if necessary; dilute fungicidal sprays by one-third when temperatures rise above 85°F/29°C.

- ☐ Plant out hot-weather herbs, such as basil and rosemary.

SUMMER

Now the summer came to pass

And flowers through the grass

Joyously sprang

While all the tribes of birds sang.

—Walther Von Der Vogelweide (c. 1160–1230), *Dream Song*

Soon will the high Midsummer
pomps come on,
Soon will the musk carnations
break and swell,

Soon shall we have gold-dusted
snapdragon,
Sweet–William with his
homely cottage-smell,
And stocks in fragrant blow;

Roses that down the alleys shine afar,
And open, jasmine-muffled lattices,
And groups under the dreaming
garden-trees,

And the full moon, and the white
evening-star.

—Matthew Arnold
Thyrsis

I SHOULD LIKE TO
ENJOY THIS SUMMER
FLOWER BY FLOWER,
AS IF IT WERE TO
BE THE LAST ONE
FOR ME.

—André Gide
Journals

WATER-CONSERVING IRRIGATION

Install a drip irrigation system among shrubs, vegetables, and flower beds, and you may reduce water usage by one-half or more. Kits are available.

Water infrequently—once a week or less—but water deeply, moistening the soil to a depth of 1 ft/30 cm or more. An easy way to test how deeply you have watered is to push a steel rod into the irrigated soil. It will slip easily through moistened soil and stick when it reaches soil that is still dry.

If you have an automatic lawn sprinkler system, consider installing a rain sensor. The device shuts down the sprinkler system during periods when the weather is naturally wet. The relatively inexpensive sensor will soon pay for itself, by preventing the wastage of water. What's more, your turf will be healthier because it won't be overwatered.

Watering in the early morning, when the air is still and the sun is not strong, can greatly reduce water wasted through evaporation. (On a sunny, breezy afternoon, half of the droplets shot from a sprinkler may evaporate before they hit the ground.)

Wherever possible, surround plants with a 2–3-in/5–8 cm-deep layer of some organic mulch, such as shredded bark or leaves. This can reduce the need for summertime irrigation by half.

Drought-Resistant Plants
—— how to recognize them ——

One of the best ways to conserve water through summertime droughts is to landscape with plants that do not mind long periods of dry weather. Plants that tolerate relatively low levels of moisture are a remarkably diverse group, ranging from delicate ferns and wildflowers to shrubs and stately trees. Certain characteristics, however, are reliable clues that the plant that exhibits them can cope with prolonged drought. If you learn to recognize these characteristics, you will be able to identify which plants are the most droughtproof.

THICK, FLESHY LEAVES AND STEMS OR THICK, FLESHY ROOTS
are reservoirs in which the plant stores water.

LIGHT GRAY OR SILVERY FOLIAGE
reflects sunlight and helps keep the plant cool even during the peak of summer.

FUZZY OR DOWNY FOLIAGE
has a coat of tiny hairs over leaves and stems that serves as a sunscreen for the plant.

LEATHERY, GLOSSY LEAVES
have a thick, waxy coat that helps protect the leaves against dehydration.

FINE OR LACY FOLIAGE
is helpful because smaller leaves lose less water. (Plants "sweat" through their leaves.)

AROMATIC FOLIAGE
is a shared characteristic of herbs and other plants that thrive in regions with chronic drought.

THE SHADY GARDEN
—— *welcome relief from the hot sun* ——

Many gardeners like to relax in the shade in summertime. The following is a list of fast-growing annual flowers that can add color to a favorite retreat. (Unless otherwise noted, these plants are best adapted to areas of partial shade.)

ANNUAL FOXGLOVE (*Digitalis purpurea* 'Foxy') — white, pink, magenta

COSMOS (*Cosmos bipinnatus*) — white, pink, crimson

FLOWERING TOBACCO (*Nicotiana alata*) — white, pink, purple, green

GARDEN COLEUS (*Coleus* x *hybridus*) — mixed red, green, orange, yellow, purple foliage

NASTURTIUM (*Tropaeolum majus*) — yellow, red, orange

NEW GUINEA IMPATIENS (*Impatiens* 'New Guinea')— variegated foliage; red to pinkish purple flowers; good for deep shade

SPIDER FLOWER (*Cleome hasslerana*) — pink, purple, white

SWEET ALYSSUM (*Lobularia maritima*) — lilac, pink, purple, white

SWEET WILLIAM (*Dianthus barbatus*) — red, rose, rose-purple, white

WAX BEGONIA (*Begonia* x *semperflorens-cultorum*) — bronze green foliage; white, pink, red flowers; good for deep shade

WISHBONE FLOWER (*Torenia fournieri*) — purple-and-blue, white-and-blue, or white-and-pink, all with yellow throats

Cool-Weather Crops
— *to sow in the hottest weather* —

Midsummer brings the hottest weather to Northern gardens, yet this is the time to make a second planting of cool-season vegetables (see list below). Started now, these plants will flourish during fall's cooler weather, and insects and weeds will be less troublesome than in the springtime. In the South, the second planting should be made in early fall.

Seeds of many cool-weather crops (notably lettuce) do not germinate well in hot, dry soils. After making a midsummer or early fall sowing, water the rows well and cover them with thick, wide boards. Check under the boards daily and remove them as soon as the seedlings start to emerge from the soil.

BEETS ▪ BROCCOLI ▪ BUSH BEANS ▪
CABBAGE ▪ CARROTS ▪ CHINESE CABBAGE ▪
KALE ▪ KOHLRABI ▪ LETTUCE ▪ PEAS ▪
SWISS CHARD ▪ TURNIPS

Weather _____

Soil Conditions _____

In Bloom _____

_____

Flower Garden _____

Trees & Shrubs _____

Lawn _____

Fruits & Vegetables _____

_____

Notes _____

_____

C H E C K L I S T

COLD

- ❏ Sow beans, cucumbers, squashes, and other warm-weather crops as soon as soil in the garden warms.

- ❏ Trim juniper, yew, and hemlock hedges.

TEMPERATE

- ❏ Apply acid fertilizer to magnolias, rhododendrons, hollies, and other acid-loving plants.

- ❏ Sow seeds directly into the garden for warm-weather annuals: marigolds, zinnias, and nasturtiums.

Weather _____

Soil Conditions _____

In Bloom _____

_____

Flower Garden _____

Trees & Shrubs _____

Lawn _____

Fruits & Vegetables _____

_____

Notes _____

_____

WARM

- ❏ Prune evergreen shrubs and hedges to control shape and promote compact growth.
- ❏ Prune old garden roses and once-blooming modern shrub roses after bloom ends.

HOT

- ❏ Prune hedges and small shrubs; fertilize all shrubs and trees.
- ❏ Cover unplanted beds with clear plastic over the summer to "solarize" soil, ridding it of weeds and diseases.

Weather _____

Soil Conditions _____

In Bloom _____

_____

Flower Garden _____

Trees & Shrubs _____

Lawn _____

Fruits & Vegetables _____

_____

Notes _____

_____

C H E C K L I S T

COLD

❑ Sow seeds of warm-weather annuals, such as marigolds, zinnias, and nasturtiums, directly into garden.

❑ Apply summer mulch to flower beds; pinch off fading flowers to promote longer season of bloom.

TEMPERATE

❑ Side-dress corn, tomatoes, peppers, squashes, and other heavy feeders with a complete fertilizer.

❑ Apply postemergent herbicide to lawn to control annual weeds.

❑ Cut fading blossoms from modern roses for continued flowering.

Weather _____

Soil Conditions _____

In Bloom _____

_____

Flower Garden _____

Trees & Shrubs _____

Lawn _____

Fruits & Vegetables _____

_____

Notes _____

_____

WARM

- ❏ Cut flowers early in the morning for longer-lasting arrangements.
- ❏ Sow tomato seeds indoors for a fall crop.
- ❏ Spread light application of a slow-release fertilizer on Bermuda grass.

HOT

- ❏ Irrigate roses deeply twice weekly during hot, dry weather.
- ❏ Sow tomato seeds indoors for a fall crop.

Weather _____

Soil Conditions _____

In Bloom _____

_____

Flower Garden _____

Trees & Shrubs _____

Lawn _____

Fruits & Vegetables _____

_____

Notes _____

_____

C H E C K L I S T

COLD

- ❑ Watch for spider mites on annual flowers, roses, junipers, and other shrubs; spray with insecticidal soap as necessary.
- ❑ Prune old garden and once-blooming shrub roses after flowers fade.

TEMPERATE

- ❑ Apply foliar fertilizer to new shrubs and trees if they start to drop their leaves.
- ❑ Order bulbs for fall planting.

Weather _____

Soil Conditions _____

In Bloom _____

_____

Flower Garden _____

Trees & Shrubs _____

Lawn _____

Fruits & Vegetables _____

_____

Notes _____

_____

WARM

- ❏ Cut back tired annuals and rejuvenate with an application of a water-soluble fertilizer.
- ❏ Water roses deeply twice weekly during hot, dry weather; fertilize with complete fertilizer.

HOT

- ❏ Watch palms for yellowing fronds—a sign of nutrient deficiencies or pests.
- ❏ Pinch back fall-blooming perennials to promote compact growth and extra blooms.

Weather _____

Soil Conditions _____

In Bloom _____

_____

Flower Garden _____

Trees & Shrubs _____

Lawn _____

Fruits & Vegetables _____

_____

Notes _____

_____

C H E C K L I S T

COLD

- ❏ Sow seed for fall crops, such as cabbage and kale, directly in the garden or set out transplants.

- ❏ Sharpen your mower blade; grass cut with a dull blade is susceptible to disease and insect damage.

TEMPERATE

- ❏ Watch roses for spider mites and spray if necessary; dilute fungicidal sprays by one-third when temperatures rise above 85°F/29°C.

- ❏ Check mower blade and sharpen it if dull. Set it 1/2 in/1.3 cm higher during hot, dry periods.

Weather _____

Soil Conditions _____

In Bloom _____

_____

Flower Garden _____

Trees & Shrubs _____

Lawn _____

Fruits & Vegetables _____

_____

Notes _____

_____

WARM

- ❏ Use floating row covers to protect vegetable plants from heat and pests.
- ❏ Set out tomato transplants for a fall crop.
- ❏ Sharpen mower blade and then set it 1/2 in/1.3 cm higher.

HOT

- ❏ Plant heat-tolerant vegetables, such as calabaza squash and yard-long beans.
- ❏ If watering is restricted, let lawn go dormant; it will likely green up when rains return; raise mower blade 1/2 in/1.3 cm.

AUGUST

Weather _____

Soil Conditions _____

In Bloom _____

_____

Flower Garden _____

Trees & Shrubs _____

Lawn _____

Fruits & Vegetables _____

_____

Notes _____

_____

C　H　E　C　K　L　I　S　T

COLD

❏ Cut back tired annuals and rejuvenate with soluble fertilizer.

❏ Divide and transplant bearded irises and Madonna lilies.

TEMPERATE

❏ Pruning trees or shrubs now prompts soft new growth that will be vulnerable to frost damage.

❏ Plant autumn-flowering crocuses and colchicums.

Weather _____

Soil Conditions _____

In Bloom _____

_____

Flower Garden _____

Trees & Shrubs _____

Lawn _____

Fruits & Vegetables _____

_____

Notes _____

_____

WARM

- ❏ Prune seed heads from crape myrtles to encourage a fall bloom.
- ❏ Sow seeds of annuals indoors for fall transplants.

HOT

- ❏ Cut back bougainvillea and other rampant shrubs.
- ❏ Sow annual seeds for fall transplants.

Weather _____

Soil Conditions _____

In Bloom _____

_____

Flower Garden _____

Trees & Shrubs _____

Lawn _____

Fruits & Vegetables _____

_____

Notes _____

_____

C H E C K L I S T

COLD

- ❏ Stop fertilizing and deadheading roses, to help prepare them for winter dormancy.

- ❏ As weather cools, plant heat-sensitive crops, such as lettuce, spinach, and peas.

TEMPERATE

- ❏ Stop fertilizing and deadheading roses; order bare-root roses for fall planting.

- ❏ Plant fall crops of heat-sensitive plants, such as kale, lettuce, and peas.

Weather _____

Soil Conditions _____

In Bloom _____

_____

Flower Garden _____

Trees & Shrubs _____

Lawn _____

Fruits & Vegetables _____

_____

Notes _____

_____

WARM

- ❏ Fertilize summer-flowering bulbs with a 5-10-5 fertilizer.
- ❏ Plant peas and bush beans.

HOT

- ❏ Plant Dutch iris, freesia, Madonna lily, and other fall and winter-flowering bulbs.
- ❏ Shorten rose canes by one-third for a better bloom in fall.

FALL

I'm going out to clean the pasture spring;

I'll only stop to rake the leaves away

(And wait to watch the water clear, I may):

I shan't be gone long.—You come too.

—Robert Frost, *The Pasture*

"Do bulbs live a long time?..."

inquired Mary anxiously.

"They're things as helps themselves,"

said Martha.

"...If you don't trouble 'em,

most of 'em'll work away

underground for a lifetime

an' spread out an' have

little 'uns."

—Frances Hodgson Burnett
The Secret Garden

LISTEN!
THE WIND IS RISING,
AND THE AIR IS WILD
WITH LEAVES,

WE HAVE HAD OUR
SUMMER EVENINGS,
NOW FOR
OCTOBER EVES!

—Humbert Wolfe
Autumn (Resignation)

A Harbinger of Frost

Look for the arrival of the first hard frost on a windless, clear night. On overcast nights clouds act as insulation, mitigating the effects of lower temperatures.

Fall Secrets for Vegetables

For the biggest, best-flavored garlic bulbs next summer, plant in fall. Set individual cloves with their tips 2 in/ 5 cm below the surface in well-drained soil. For the earliest spring lettuces in northern areas, sow a cold-hardy cultivar such as 'Winter Marvel' one month before the expected date of the first fall frost. When the ground freezes, cover seedlings with a floating row-cover (a special permeable plastic fabric, which is available at most garden centers).

Feeding in Fall

Late fall is an excellent time to fertilize trees and shrubs, since their roots continue to collect nutrients even after cold weather stops growth above ground. A fall feeding prepares the plants for more vigorous growth in the spring.

Bulbs for Naturalizing
—— *flowers for carefree gardening* ——

If planted in an informal setting, some types of bulbs perform as true perennials—they "naturalize," blooming year after year, and even reproducing themselves. Here are some bulbs suited to this most carefree kind of gardening; all of them should be planted in the fall.

In Meadows or Unmowed Grass

Camass *(Camassia quamash)*
blue, white; spring; requires moist soil; best in Mountain West

Crocus *(Crocus* spp.)
mixed or solid blue, purple, white, yellow; early spring

Daffodil, jonquil, narcissus *(Narcissus* spp.)
yellow, white, orange, often bi-colored; cultivars of trumpet, large cup; double daffodil types generally successful in the North; *N. jonquilla* x *odorus* 'Campernelle' flourishes in the Deep South

Species tulips *(Tulipa tarda, T. humilis, T. linifolia)*
mixed or solid red, yellow, lilac, white; mid to late spring; most successful in Western prairie states

In Lawns

Crocus *(Crocus tomasinianus)*
lilac to purple; early spring

Glory-of-the-snow *(Chionodoxa luciliae)*
blue, white; late winter to early spring

Siberian squill *(Scilla siberica)*
blue; early spring

Colorful Fall Foliage
— *trees and shrubs for Northern gardens* —

Yellow Foliage

BIRCH (*Betula* spp.)

BITTERSWEET (*Celastrus* spp.)

BOWER ACTINIDIA (*Actinidia arguta*)

FRINGE TREE (*Chionanthus virginicus*)

GINKGO (*Ginkgo biloba*)

TRIFOLIATE ORANGE (*Poncirus trifoliata*)

REDBUD (*Cercis* spp.)

STAR MAGNOLIA (*Magnolia stellata*)

SUMMERSWEET (*Clethra alnifolia*)

WITCH HAZEL (*Hamamelis* spp.)

Red Foliage

BLACK TUPELO (*Nyssa sylvatica*)

BRIDAL WREATH (*Spiraea prunifolia*)

FOTHERGILLA (*Fothergilla* spp.)

FRANKLINIA (*Franklinia alatamaha*)

JAPANESE MAPLE (*Acer japonicum*)

KOREAN STEWARTIA (*Stewartia koreana*)

SOURWOOD (*Oxydendrum aboreum*)

SWEET GUM (*Liquidambar styraciflua*)

VIBURNUM—deciduous species (*Viburnum* spp.)

VIRGINIA CREEPER, BOSTON IVY (*Parthenocissus* spp.)

FALL FLOWERS

—— *trees and shrubs in mild-winter regions* ——

BLUE HIBISCUS *(Alyogyne huegelii)*
blue to deep purple

BIRD OF PARADISE *(Caesalpinia)*
yellow to red

CAMELLIA *(Camellia sasanqua)*
white to dark red

ESCALLONIA *(Escallonia* spp.)
white, red, pink

FLOSS-SILK TREE *(Chorisia* spp.)
white, yellow, pink, purplish red

FUCHSIA *(Fuchsia* spp.)
mixed and solid purple, violet, red, pink, white

HONG KONG ORCHID TREE *(Bauhinia blakeana)*
blue to deep purple

LEMON-FLOWERED GUM *(Eucalyptus woodwardii)*
pale yellow

RED CAP GUM *(Eucalyptus erythrocorys)*
red-and-yellow

TREE MALLOW *(Lavatera* spp.)
lavender, pink, white

SEPTEMBER

Weather _____

Soil Conditions _____

In Bloom _____

_____

Flower Garden _____

Trees & Shrubs _____

Lawn _____

Fruits & Vegetables _____

_____

Notes _____

_____

C H E C K L I S T

COLD

- ❑ To prolong bloom, protect tender annuals from early frosts by covering them with a plastic drop cloth.

- ❑ Divide and replant overgrown or crowded perennial flowers.

- ❑ Plant spring-flowering bulbs.

TEMPERATE

- ❑ Apply 3–4 in/8–10 cm inches of mulch around trees and shrubs to protect them from drying winter winds.

- ❑ Pinch off new tomato flowers to promote ripening of existing fruits before frost.

Weather _____

Soil Conditions _____

In Bloom _____

_____

Flower Garden _____

Trees & Shrubs _____

Lawn _____

Fruits & Vegetables _____

_____

Notes _____

_____

WARM

- ❏ Apply 3-1-2 fertilizer at recommended rate to Bermuda grass and zoysia lawns.
- ❏ Sow annual flower seeds for winter display.
- ❏ Apply complete fertilizer to roses as last feeding of the year.

HOT

- ❏ Treat soil around acid-loving ixoras, azaleas, and allamandas with sulfur.
- ❏ Sow annual seeds for winter display.
- ❏ Divide and replant overgrown bulb clumps before fall and winter rains.

SEPTEMBER
WEEK 3

Weather _____

Soil Conditions _____

In Bloom _____

_____

Flower Garden _____

Trees & Shrubs _____

Lawn _____

Fruits & Vegetables _____

_____

Notes _____

_____

C H E C K L I S T

COLD

❏ Apply 3-1-2 fertilizer to lawn. Add powdered limestone if pH test reveals acid soil.

❏ Water roses deeply during any hot weather; watch for return of mildew on foliage.

TEMPERATE

❏ Divide and replant overgrown or crowded perennials; plant lilies as soon as bulbs are available.

❏ Resume spraying roses with full-strength fungicides.

❏ Plant cover crop of oats or rye in vacated vegetable garden beds.

SEPTEMBER

WEEK 4

Weather _____

Soil Conditions _____

In Bloom _____

_____

Flower Garden _____

Trees & Shrubs _____

Lawn _____

Fruits & Vegetables _____

_____

Notes _____

_____

WARM

- ❏ Plant paperwhite narcissus, bulbous iris, spider lily, ranunculus, and fall-blooming crocus.
- ❏ Set out transplants of cool-weather vegetables, such as lettuce, mustard, kale, turnips, cabbage, Swiss chard, and broccoli.

HOT

- ❏ Prune and fertilize roses.
- ❏ Sow seeds in garden of winter crops: lettuce, mustard, kale, turnips, cabbage, Swiss chard, and broccoli.
- ❏ Plant potatoes for fall crop.

SEPTEMBER
NOTES

_____

_____

_____

_____

_____

_____

_____

_____

_____

C H E C K L I S T

COLD

- ❏ Make final plantings of fast-maturing crops, such as radishes and lettuce.
- ❏ Remember that fall is an excellent time for planting perennial flowers.
- ❏ Check nurseries for sales on trees and shrubs—fall is an excellent season for planting.

TEMPERATE

- ❏ Apply 3-1-2 fertilizer to lawn. Add powdered limestone if pH test reveals acid soil.
- ❏ Rake lawn to remove thatch and weeds. Aerate if soil seems hard and compacted.

SEPTEMBER
NOTES

_____

_____

_____

_____

_____

_____

_____

_____

_____

WARM

❑ Blackened twigs on fruit trees may be a symptom of fire blight. Cut off infected branches.

❑ Plant potatoes for fall crop.

❑ Overseed Bermuda grass with perennial rye grass to keep lawn green through the winter.

HOT

❑ Sow perennial seeds for late-winter and spring plantings.

❑ Apply 3-1-2 fertilizer at recommended rate to St. Augustine, Bahia, and centipede grasses.

OCTOBER

Weather _____

Soil Conditions _____

In Bloom _____

_____

Flower Garden _____

Trees & Shrubs _____

Lawn _____

Fruits & Vegetables _____

_____

Notes _____

_____

C H E C K L I S T

COLD

❏ Take cuttings of tender plants in outdoor tubs and boxes to over-winter indoors.

❏ Remove frost-killed annuals. Turn soil, adding organic matter, lime, and fertilizer as needed.

TEMPERATE

❏ Continue plantings of trees and shrubs.

❏ Take cuttings of annuals, such as coleus or impatiens, to be over-wintered indoors.

❏ Plant spring bulbs.

Weather _____

Soil Conditions _____

In Bloom _____

_____

Flower Garden _____

Trees & Shrubs _____

Lawn _____

Fruits & Vegetables _____

_____

Notes _____

_____

WARM

- ❏ Plant trees and shrubs.
- ❏ Mulch existing tree and shrub plantings with fallen leaves or pine straw.
- ❏ Divide and replant overgrown or crowded perennials.

HOT

- ❏ Fertilize citrus trees and all shrubs.
- ❏ Apply 3–4 in/8–10 cm of organic mulch around tree and shrub plantings.
- ❏ Sow annual flower seeds for winter display.

OCTOBER

Weather _____

Soil Conditions _____

In Bloom _____

_____

Flower Garden _____

Trees & Shrubs _____

Lawn _____

Fruits & Vegetables _____

_____

Notes _____

_____

C H E C K L I S T

COLD

❏ Move all insecticides and other garden chemicals to a frost-free storage area.

❏ Rake up, bag, and dispose of fallen rose leaves off-site.

❏ Plant garlic sets now and blanket with mulch after the ground freezes.

TEMPERATE

❏ Plant spinach and garlic.

❏ Plant out ornamental cabbages and kales for winter displays.

❏ Plant bare-root roses.

OCTOBER

Weather _____

Soil Conditions _____

In Bloom _____

_____

Flower Garden _____

Trees & Shrubs _____

Lawn _____

Fruits & Vegetables _____

_____

Notes _____

_____

WARM

- ❏ Plant all spring-flowering bulbs.
- ❏ Foliar-feed roses with dilute fertilizer to promote better fall bloom.
- ❏ Watch for cabbage loopers—spray with biological insecticide Bt.

HOT

- ❏ Sow seeds of sweet alyssum in rose beds to provide living, flowering mulch.
- ❏ Direct-seed cool-weather vegetables, such as lettuce, mustard, turnips, cabbage, and broccoli.

C H E C K L I S T

COLD

- ❏ Shred piles of fall leaves with the lawn mower; bag and store for use as mulch next year.

- ❏ Sprinkle perennial beds with high-phosphate fertilizer to promote strong root growth.

TEMPERATE

- ❏ Collect and shred with mower fallen leaves; store in bags for next year's mulch.

- ❏ Aerate lawn to improve water absorption.

OCTOBER

N O T E S

_____

_____

_____

_____

_____

_____

_____

_____

_____

WARM

- ❏ Set out transplants of cool-weather vegetables: kale, collards, mustard, broccoli, etc.
- ❏ Apply preemergent herbicide to control annual weeds in established Bermuda grass lawns.

HOT

- ❏ Plant out new tomato seedlings.
- ❏ Lower mower blade half an inch.
- ❏ Plant window boxes and outdoor containers with calendulas, pansies, stocks, and other cool-season flowers.

Weather _____

Soil Conditions _____

In Bloom _____

_____

Flower Garden _____

Trees & Shrubs _____

Lawn _____

Fruits & Vegetables _____

_____

Notes _____

_____

C H E C K L I S T

COLD

❏ Spray evergreen shrubs with an antitranspirant to reduce winter damage to foliage.

❏ Water trees and shrubs thoroughly before the ground freezes.

TEMPERATE

❏ Prune overgrown hollies by cutting back top branches to stubs. Use prunings as holiday decorations.

❏ Rake up and dispose of rose leaves to eliminate overwintering disease spores and insect eggs.

Weather _____

Soil Conditions _____

In Bloom _____

_____

Flower Garden _____

Trees & Shrubs _____

Lawn _____

Fruits & Vegetables _____

_____

Notes _____

_____

WARM

- ❏ Protect tender plants from occasional frost to prolong bloom.
- ❏ Fill in perennial beds with annual flowers for winter display.

HOT

- ❏ Prune any storm-damaged trees and shrubs.
- ❏ Plant agapanthus, amaryllis, montbretia, tigridia, watsonia, and lily bulbs for spring and summer bloom.

Weather _____

Soil Conditions _____

In Bloom _____

_____

Flower Garden _____

Trees & Shrubs _____

Lawn _____

Fruits & Vegetables _____

_____

Notes _____

_____

C H E C K L I S T

COLD

❑ Protect cold-sensitive roses by covering them with "rose cones" or by hilling soil around their bases.

❑ Clean up perennial beds and add debris to the compost heap.

TEMPERATE

❑ Prepare empty flower and vegetable beds for spring planting. Turn the soil and mix in compost or some other organic matter.

❑ Winter-protect sensitive roses by hilling up soil around the bases or by covering bushes with plastic-foam "rose cones."

NOVEMBER
WEEK 4

Weather _____

Soil Conditions _____

In Bloom _____

_____

Flower Garden _____

Trees & Shrubs _____

Lawn _____

Fruits & Vegetables _____

_____

Notes _____

_____

WARM

❑ Foliar-feed fall vegetables and herbs with a water-soluble fertilizer.

❑ Water lawn if weather is dry.

HOT

❑ Apply postemergent broadleaf weed control to lawn at recommended rate.

❑ Plant vacant vegetable beds with cover crop of oats or rye.

Plant name _____

❏ *Annual*   ❏ *Perennial*   ❏ *Bulb*   ❏ *Shrub*   ❏ *Tree*
❏ *Seed*   ❏ *Bare-rooted*   ❏ *Balled-and-burlapped*   ❏ *Container-grown*

Where purchased _____

Date received _____   *Condition upon arrival* _____

Where planted _____

Height at maturity _____   *Spread at maturity* _____

Season and color of bloom _____

How it performed _____

Plant name _____

❏ *Annual*   ❏ *Perennial*   ❏ *Bulb*   ❏ *Shrub*   ❏ *Tree*
❏ *Seed*   ❏ *Bare-rooted*   ❏ *Balled-and-burlapped*   ❏ *Container-grown*

Where purchased _____

Date received _____   *Condition upon arrival* _____

Where planted _____

Height at maturity _____   *Spread at maturity* _____

Season and color of bloom _____

How it performed _____

Plant name _____

❑ Annual   ❑ Perennial   ❑ Bulb   ❑ Shrub   ❑ Tree
❑ Seed   ❑ Bare-rooted   ❑ Balled-and-burlapped   ❑ Container-grown

Where purchased _____

Date received _____ Condition upon arrival _____

Where planted _____

Height at maturity _____ Spread at maturity _____

Season and color of bloom _____

How it performed _____

Plant name _____

❑ Annual   ❑ Perennial   ❑ Bulb   ❑ Shrub   ❑ Tree
❑ Seed   ❑ Bare-rooted   ❑ Balled-and-burlapped   ❑ Container-grown

Where purchased _____

Date received _____ Condition upon arrival _____

Where planted _____

Height at maturity _____ Spread at maturity _____

Season and color of bloom _____

How it performed _____

PLANT PROFILES

Plant name _____

❏ *Annual*   ❏ *Perennial*   ❏ *Bulb*   ❏ *Shrub*   ❏ *Tree*
❏ *Seed*   ❏ *Bare-rooted*   ❏ *Balled-and-burlapped*   ❏ *Container-grown*

Where purchased _____

Date received _____   *Condition upon arrival* _____

Where planted _____

Height at maturity _____   *Spread at maturity* _____

Season and color of bloom _____

How it performed _____

Plant name _____

❏ *Annual*   ❏ *Perennial*   ❏ *Bulb*   ❏ *Shrub*   ❏ *Tree*
❏ *Seed*   ❏ *Bare-rooted*   ❏ *Balled-and-burlapped*   ❏ *Container-grown*

Where purchased _____

Date received _____   *Condition upon arrival* _____

Where planted _____

Height at maturity _____   *Spread at maturity* _____

Season and color of bloom _____

How it performed _____

Plant name _____

❏ *Annual*   ❏ *Perennial*   ❏ *Bulb*   ❏ *Shrub*   ❏ *Tree*
❏ *Seed*   ❏ *Bare-rooted*   ❏ *Balled-and-burlapped*   ❏ *Container-grown*

Where purchased _____

Date received _____   *Condition upon arrival* _____

Where planted _____

Height at maturity _____   *Spread at maturity* _____

Season and color of bloom _____

How it performed _____

Plant name _____

❏ *Annual*   ❏ *Perennial*   ❏ *Bulb*   ❏ *Shrub*   ❏ *Tree*
❏ *Seed*   ❏ *Bare-rooted*   ❏ *Balled-and-burlapped*   ❏ *Container-grown*

Where purchased _____

Date received _____   *Condition upon arrival* _____

Where planted _____

Height at maturity _____   *Spread at maturity* _____

Season and color of bloom _____

How it performed _____

PLANT PROFILES

Plant name _____

❏ Annual   ❏ Perennial   ❏ Bulb   ❏ Shrub   ❏ Tree

❏ Seed   ❏ Bare-rooted   ❏ Balled-and-burlapped   ❏ Container-grown

Where purchased _____

Date received _____ Condition upon arrival _____

Where planted _____

Height at maturity _____ Spread at maturity _____

Season and color of bloom _____

How it performed _____

Plant name _____

❏ Annual   ❏ Perennial   ❏ Bulb   ❏ Shrub   ❏ Tree

❏ Seed   ❏ Bare-rooted   ❏ Balled-and-burlapped   ❏ Container-grown

Where purchased _____

Date received _____ Condition upon arrival _____

Where planted _____

Height at maturity _____ Spread at maturity _____

Season and color of bloom _____

How it performed _____

Plant name _____

❑ Annual   ❑ Perennial   ❑ Bulb   ❑ Shrub   ❑ Tree
❑ Seed   ❑ Bare-rooted   ❑ Balled-and-burlapped   ❑ Container-grown

Where purchased _____

Date received _____   Condition upon arrival _____

Where planted _____

Height at maturity _____   Spread at maturity _____

Season and color of bloom _____

How it performed _____

Plant name _____

❑ Annual   ❑ Perennial   ❑ Bulb   ❑ Shrub   ❑ Tree
❑ Seed   ❑ Bare-rooted   ❑ Balled-and-burlapped   ❑ Container-grown

Where purchased _____

Date received _____   Condition upon arrival _____

Where planted _____

Height at maturity _____   Spread at maturity _____

Season and color of bloom _____

How it performed _____

PLANT PROFILES

Plant name _____

❏ Annual   ❏ Perennial   ❏ Bulb   ❏ Shrub   ❏ Tree
❏ Seed   ❏ Bare-rooted   ❏ Balled-and-burlapped   ❏ Container-grown

Where purchased _____

Date received _____   Condition upon arrival _____

Where planted _____

Height at maturity _____   Spread at maturity _____

Season and color of bloom _____

How it performed _____

Plant name _____

❏ Annual   ❏ Perennial   ❏ Bulb   ❏ Shrub   ❏ Tree
❏ Seed   ❏ Bare-rooted   ❏ Balled-and-burlapped   ❏ Container-grown

Where purchased _____

Date received _____   Condition upon arrival _____

Where planted _____

Height at maturity _____   Spread at maturity _____

Season and color of bloom _____

How it performed _____

Plant name _____

❏ *Annual*　　　❏ *Perennial*　　　❏ *Bulb*　　　❏ *Shrub*　　　❏ *Tree*
❏ *Seed*　　❏ *Bare-rooted*　　❏ *Balled-and-burlapped*　　❏ *Container-grown*

Where purchased _____

Date received _____　*Condition upon arrival* _____

Where planted _____

Height at maturity _____　*Spread at maturity* _____

Season and color of bloom _____

How it performed _____

Plant name _____

❏ *Annual*　　　❏ *Perennial*　　　❏ *Bulb*　　　❏ *Shrub*　　　❏ *Tree*
❏ *Seed*　　❏ *Bare-rooted*　　❏ *Balled-and-burlapped*　　❏ *Container-grown*

Where purchased _____

Date received _____　*Condition upon arrival* _____

Where planted _____

Height at maturity _____　*Spread at maturity* _____

Season and color of bloom _____

How it performed _____

PLANT PROFILES

Plant name _____

❑ Annual   ❑ Perennial   ❑ Bulb   ❑ Shrub   ❑ Tree

❑ Seed   ❑ Bare-rooted   ❑ Balled-and-burlapped   ❑ Container-grown

Where purchased _____

Date received _____ Condition upon arrival _____

Where planted _____

Height at maturity _____ Spread at maturity _____

Season and color of bloom _____

How it performed _____

Plant name _____

❑ Annual   ❑ Perennial   ❑ Bulb   ❑ Shrub   ❑ Tree

❑ Seed   ❑ Bare-rooted   ❑ Balled-and-burlapped   ❑ Container-grown

Where purchased _____

Date received _____ Condition upon arrival _____

Where planted _____

Height at maturity _____ Spread at maturity _____

Season and color of bloom _____

How it performed _____

Plant name _____

❏ *Annual*   ❏ *Perennial*   ❏ *Bulb*   ❏ *Shrub*   ❏ *Tree*
❏ *Seed*   ❏ *Bare-rooted*   ❏ *Balled-and-burlapped*   ❏ *Container-grown*

Where purchased _____

Date received _____   *Condition upon arrival* _____

Where planted _____

Height at maturity _____   *Spread at maturity* _____

Season and color of bloom _____

How it performed _____

Plant name _____

❏ *Annual*   ❏ *Perennial*   ❏ *Bulb*   ❏ *Shrub*   ❏ *Tree*
❏ *Seed*   ❏ *Bare-rooted*   ❏ *Balled-and-burlapped*   ❏ *Container-grown*

Where purchased _____

Date received _____   *Condition upon arrival* _____

Where planted _____

Height at maturity _____   *Spread at maturity* _____

Season and color of bloom _____

How it performed _____

PLANT PROFILES

Plant name _____

❏ Annual   ❏ Perennial   ❏ Bulb   ❏ Shrub   ❏ Tree
❏ Seed   ❏ Bare-rooted   ❏ Balled-and-burlapped   ❏ Container-grown

Where purchased _____

Date received _____   Condition upon arrival _____

Where planted _____

Height at maturity _____   Spread at maturity _____

Season and color of bloom _____

How it performed _____

Plant name _____

❏ Annual   ❏ Perennial   ❏ Bulb   ❏ Shrub   ❏ Tree
❏ Seed   ❏ Bare-rooted   ❏ Balled-and-burlapped   ❏ Container-grown

Where purchased _____

Date received _____   Condition upon arrival _____

Where planted _____

Height at maturity _____   Spread at maturity _____

Season and color of bloom _____

How it performed _____

Plant name _____

❏ *Annual*   ❏ *Perennial*   ❏ *Bulb*   ❏ *Shrub*   ❏ *Tree*
❏ *Seed*   ❏ *Bare-rooted*   ❏ *Balled-and-burlapped*   ❏ *Container-grown*

Where purchased _____

Date received _____   *Condition upon arrival* _____

Where planted _____

Height at maturity _____   *Spread at maturity* _____

Season and color of bloom _____

How it performed _____

Plant name _____

❏ *Annual*   ❏ *Perennial*   ❏ *Bulb*   ❏ *Shrub*   ❏ *Tree*
❏ *Seed*   ❏ *Bare-rooted*   ❏ *Balled-and-burlapped*   ❏ *Container-grown*

Where purchased _____

Date received _____   *Condition upon arrival* _____

Where planted _____

Height at maturity _____   *Spread at maturity* _____

Season and color of bloom _____

How it performed _____

Crop _____

Cultivar_____ Date planted _____

❏ Annual ❏ Perennial ❏ Bush ❏ Tree ❏ Vine
❏ Seed ❏ Seedling ❏ Bare-rooted ❏ Balled-and-burlapped ❏ Container

Source _____

Where planted _____

Feeding_____ Problems_____

Date of harvest _____ Yield _____

Quality _____

Crop _____

Cultivar_____ Date planted _____

❏ Annual ❏ Perennial ❏ Bush ❏ Tree ❏ Vine
❏ Seed ❏ Seedling ❏ Bare-rooted ❏ Balled-and-burlapped ❏ Container

Source _____

Where planted _____

Feeding_____ Problems_____

Date of harvest _____ Yield _____

Quality _____

Crop _____

*Cultivar*_____ *Date planted* _____

❏ *Annual*　　❏ *Perennial*　　❏ *Bush*　　❏ *Tree*　　❏ *Vine*
❏ *Seed*　❏ *Seedling*　❏ *Bare-rooted*　❏ *Balled-and-burlapped*　❏ *Container*

Source _____

Where planted _____

*Feeding*_____　*Problems*_____

Date of harvest _____　*Yield* _____

Quality _____

Crop _____

*Cultivar*_____ *Date planted* _____

❏ *Annual*　　❏ *Perennial*　　❏ *Bush*　　❏ *Tree*　　❏ *Vine*
❏ *Seed*　❏ *Seedling*　❏ *Bare-rooted*　❏ *Balled-and-burlapped*　❏ *Container*

Source _____

Where planted _____

*Feeding*_____　*Problems*_____

Date of harvest _____　*Yield* _____

Quality _____

FRUIT & VEGETABLE PROFILES

Crop _____

Cultivar_____ Date planted _____

❏ Annual ❏ Perennial ❏ Bush ❏ Tree ❏ Vine
❏ Seed ❏ Seedling ❏ Bare-rooted ❏ Balled-and-burlapped ❏ Container

Source _____

Where planted _____

Feeding_____ Problems _____

Date of harvest _____ Yield _____

Quality _____

Crop _____

Cultivar_____ Date planted _____

❏ Annual ❏ Perennial ❏ Bush ❏ Tree ❏ Vine
❏ Seed ❏ Seedling ❏ Bare-rooted ❏ Balled-and-burlapped ❏ Container

Source _____

Where planted _____

Feeding_____ Problems _____

Date of harvest _____ Yield _____

Quality _____

Crop _____

*Cultivar*_____ *Date planted* _____

❑ *Annual*   ❑ *Perennial*   ❑ *Bush*   ❑ *Tree*   ❑ *Vine*
❑ *Seed*   ❑ *Seedling*   ❑ *Bare-rooted*   ❑ *Balled-and-burlapped*   ❑ *Container*

Source _____

Where planted _____

*Feeding*_____ *Problems*_____

Date of harvest _____ *Yield* _____

Quality _____

Crop _____

*Cultivar*_____ *Date planted* _____

❑ *Annual*   ❑ *Perennial*   ❑ *Bush*   ❑ *Tree*   ❑ *Vine*
❑ *Seed*   ❑ *Seedling*   ❑ *Bare-rooted*   ❑ *Balled-and-burlapped*   ❑ *Container*

Source _____

Where planted _____

*Feeding*_____ *Problems*_____

Date of harvest _____ *Yield* _____

Quality _____

Fruit & Vegetable Profiles

Crop _____

Cultivar_____ Date planted _____

❑ Annual   ❑ Perennial   ❑ Bush   ❑ Tree   ❑ Vine
❑ Seed   ❑ Seedling   ❑ Bare-rooted   ❑ Balled-and-burlapped   ❑ Container

Source _____

Where planted _____

Feeding_____ Problems_____

Date of harvest _____ Yield _____

Quality _____

Crop _____

Cultivar_____ Date planted _____

❑ Annual   ❑ Perennial   ❑ Bush   ❑ Tree   ❑ Vine
❑ Seed   ❑ Seedling   ❑ Bare-rooted   ❑ Balled-and-burlapped   ❑ Container

Source _____

Where planted _____

Feeding_____ Problems_____

Date of harvest _____ Yield _____

Quality _____

Crop _____

*Cultivar*_____ *Date planted* _____

❑ *Annual*   ❑ *Perennial*   ❑ *Bush*   ❑ *Tree*   ❑ *Vine*
❑ *Seed*   ❑ *Seedling*   ❑ *Bare-rooted*   ❑ *Balled-and-burlapped*   ❑ *Container*

Source _____

Where planted _____

*Feeding*_____ *Problems*_____

Date of harvest _____ *Yield* _____

Quality _____

Crop _____

*Cultivar*_____ *Date planted* _____

❑ *Annual*   ❑ *Perennial*   ❑ *Bush*   ❑ *Tree*   ❑ *Vine*
❑ *Seed*   ❑ *Seedling*   ❑ *Bare-rooted*   ❑ *Balled-and-burlapped*   ❑ *Container*

Source _____

Where planted _____

*Feeding*_____ *Problems*_____

Date of harvest _____ *Yield* _____

Quality _____

Crop _____

Cultivar_____ Date planted _____

❑ Annual ❑ Perennial ❑ Bush ❑ Tree ❑ Vine
❑ Seed ❑ Seedling ❑ Bare-rooted ❑ Balled-and-burlapped ❑ Container

Source _____

Where planted _____

Feeding_____ Problems_____

Date of harvest _____ Yield _____

Quality _____

Crop _____

Cultivar_____ Date planted _____

❑ Annual ❑ Perennial ❑ Bush ❑ Tree ❑ Vine
❑ Seed ❑ Seedling ❑ Bare-rooted ❑ Balled-and-burlapped ❑ Container

Source _____

Where planted _____

Feeding_____ Problems_____

Date of harvest _____ Yield _____

Quality _____

Crop _____

*Cultivar*_____ *Date planted* _____

❏ *Annual*　　　❏ *Perennial*　　　❏ *Bush*　　　❏ *Tree*　　　❏ *Vine*
❏ *Seed*　❏ *Seedling*　❏ *Bare-rooted*　❏ *Balled-and-burlapped*　❏ *Container*

Source _____

*Where planted*_____

*Feeding*_____ *Problems*_____

Date of harvest _____ *Yield* _____

Quality _____

Crop _____

*Cultivar*_____ *Date planted* _____

❏ *Annual*　　　❏ *Perennial*　　　❏ *Bush*　　　❏ *Tree*　　　❏ *Vine*
❏ *Seed*　❏ *Seedling*　❏ *Bare-rooted*　❏ *Balled-and-burlapped*　❏ *Container*

Source _____

*Where planted*_____

*Feeding*_____ *Problems*_____

Date of harvest _____ *Yield* _____

Quality _____

Crop _____

Cultivar_____ Date planted _____

❏ Annual ❏ Perennial ❏ Bush ❏ Tree ❏ Vine
❏ Seed ❏ Seedling ❏ Bare-rooted ❏ Balled-and-burlapped ❏ Container

Source _____

Where planted _____

Feeding_____ Problems_____

Date of harvest _____ Yield _____

Quality _____

Crop _____

Cultivar_____ Date planted _____

❏ Annual ❏ Perennial ❏ Bush ❏ Tree ❏ Vine
❏ Seed ❏ Seedling ❏ Bare-rooted ❏ Balled-and-burlapped ❏ Container

Source _____

Where planted _____

Feeding_____ Problems_____

Date of harvest _____ Yield _____

Quality _____

Crop _____

*Cultivar*_____ *Date planted* _____

❏ *Annual*   ❏ *Perennial*   ❏ *Bush*   ❏ *Tree*   ❏ *Vine*
❏ *Seed*   ❏ *Seedling*   ❏ *Bare-rooted*   ❏ *Balled-and-burlapped*   ❏ *Container*

Source _____

Where planted _____

*Feeding*_____ *Problems*_____

Date of harvest _____ *Yield* _____

Quality _____

Crop _____

*Cultivar*_____ *Date planted* _____

❏ *Annual*   ❏ *Perennial*   ❏ *Bush*   ❏ *Tree*   ❏ *Vine*
❏ *Seed*   ❏ *Seedling*   ❏ *Bare-rooted*   ❏ *Balled-and-burlapped*   ❏ *Container*

Source _____

Where planted _____

*Feeding*_____ *Problems*_____

Date of harvest _____ *Yield* _____

Quality _____

FRUIT & VEGETABLE PROFILES

Crop _____

Cultivar_____ Date planted _____

❏ Annual ❏ Perennial ❏ Bush ❏ Tree ❏ Vine
❏ Seed ❏ Seedling ❏ Bare-rooted ❏ Balled-and-burlapped ❏ Container

Source _____

Where planted _____

Feeding_____ Problems_____

Date of harvest _____ Yield _____

Quality _____

Crop _____

Cultivar_____ Date planted _____

❏ Annual ❏ Perennial ❏ Bush ❏ Tree ❏ Vine
❏ Seed ❏ Seedling ❏ Bare-rooted ❏ Balled-and-burlapped ❏ Container

Source _____

Where planted _____

Feeding_____ Problems_____

Date of harvest _____ Yield _____

Quality _____

Crop _____

Cultivar_____ Date planted _____

❏ Annual ❏ Perennial ❏ Bush ❏ Tree ❏ Vine
❏ Seed ❏ Seedling ❏ Bare-rooted ❏ Balled-and-burlapped ❏ Container

Source _____

Where planted _____

Feeding_____ Problems_____

Date of harvest _____ Yield _____

Quality _____

Crop _____

Cultivar_____ Date planted _____

❏ Annual ❏ Perennial ❏ Bush ❏ Tree ❏ Vine
❏ Seed ❏ Seedling ❏ Bare-rooted ❏ Balled-and-burlapped ❏ Container

Source _____

Where planted _____

Feeding_____ Problems_____

Date of harvest _____ Yield _____

Quality _____

WORKING WITH SOIL

The soil beneath your boots is the gardener's fundamental resource. It is what anchors plants and it is the reservoir from which they draw oxygen, water, and nutrients. The quality of your soil determines what will grow in your garden. A knowledge of its chemistry and structure should be the basis of your gardening plans and tasks. Fortunately, a few simple tests will tell you all you need to know.

Sampling the soil. The soil of a garden can vary from spot to spot. To get accurate results from a soil test, you need an accurate soil sample. To collect a truly representative sample from your garden, gather samples of 1 cup/1/4 L or more from several different areas in a bed or plot. To make sure that you will be testing soils that plant roots will actually encounter, dig down 2 in/5cm before gathering your samples. Put the samples together in a clean plastic bag and mix them by shaking. From this blend take the samples that will actually be tested.

Home soil-testing kits are available at garden centers, but more accurate results can be obtained by sending a soil sample to a public or private soil-testing laboratory. Your local Cooperative Extension Service office (included in the state or county listings in the telephone directory) will either test the soil or refer you to a lab that will conduct the test. Generally, a laboratory will provide a basic soil-management program with its analysis of your garden's pH level and the nutrients it needs.

Understanding pH. Acidity and alkalinity are measured on the pH scale, which runs from 0 (pure acid) to 14 (pure alkaline). From the neutral point of 7, the numbers increase or decrease geometrically—a pH of 5 is 10 times more acidic than a pH of 6.

Tests for texture. Gardening books often recommend plants for sandy or silty or clayey soils, and often base instructions for watering and fertilization on these classifications. To determine the texture of your soil, first take a pinch of soil from the sample you gathered and let it dry. Rub the soil between your fingertip and thumb. If the soil feels gritty, it is sandy; if it feels floury, it is silty. Next, take a handful of soil from the dry sample and moisten it slightly. If you can roll the moistened soil into a thin, flexible string, it is clayey. If the string is brittle, the soil is more likely a loam—a mixture of sand, silt, and clay.

Checking for drainage. Catalogs and nurseries recommend certain plants for well-drained soils, and they specify others that will thrive in average or even in poorly drained soils. Which term describes your soil? To find out, dig a hole 1 ft/30 cm wide and 1 ft/30 cm deep and fill it with water. If the water drains out of the hole within a few minutes, you soil is very well drained. If the water drains away within 30 minutes to an hour, your drainage is good to average. If there is still water in the bottom of the hole after 24 hours, your soil is poorly drained.

Improving the soil. One of the best ways to improve any soil is to add organic matter to it. Work 1–4 in/2.5–10 cm of rotted manure, compost, chopped leaves, or other organic matter into the soil each year. Turn the material deeply into the soil: digging the soil adds oxygen, which microorganisms need to break down organic matter and release nutrients.

STARTING FROM SEED

Warding off disease. Seedlings started indoors are vulnerable to fungal diseases such as damping-off. To protect the young plants, sow seeds only into sterilized potting soils or commercially available soilless seed-starting mixtures.

A good homemade seed-starting mix combines 2 parts peat moss with 1 part compost. Mix well and pass the blend through 1/4 in/6.4 mm wire mesh to remove most of the lumps. Add 1 tbsp/15 ml of lime per 1 gal/3.8 L of mix. Then moisten it, place it in an oven-proof pan, cover it with aluminum foil, and bake at 200°F/90°C for 35 to 45 minutes.

When sowing very fine seeds, such as those of begonias and impatiens, mix the seeds with some clean sand. The sand makes it much easier to spread the seeds evenly over the soil or seed-starting mix.

Warmth for better germination. To keep the soil warmer and promote faster, more vigorous germination, set waterproof heating pads for seedlings under pots and trays of freshly sown seed. These special heating pads are available from seed companies and at garden centers.

Germination in the dark. Seeds of cornflower, forget-me-not, coriander, delphinium, larkspur, nemesia, phlox, and many vegetables germinate only in darkness. Cover seed trays and pots with sheets of newspaper until the seedlings emerge.

Buying Flowering Plants

Many of the same principles hold true for buying both annuals and perennials. Below is a checklist for both types of garden plants, plus a few tips on buying bulbs.

Annuals and Perennials

❑ Select sturdy, compact plants with rich, dark green leaves.

❑ Search stems and the undersides of leaves for evidence of insects or insect eggs—the pests you bring home with you can spread through the garden.

❑ For annuals, avoid tall, lanky seedlings and seedlings that are already in bloom. Transplants that are coming into bud will adapt more quickly and easily to the move into your garden. Look for roots emerging from drainage holes at the bottoms of plastic packs or pots—this is evidence that the plants have been in the container too long and as a result may be stunted.

❑ For perennials, slip plants out of their containers. Roots growing around the exterior of the potting soil means that the plants have been in the container too long and are likely to be stunted.

Bulbs

❑ Select bulbs that are free of mold and bruises.

❑ Don't forget to browse through mail-order catalogs. Bulbs from these warehouses are usually stored in precisely controlled conditions, at the proper temperature, and with the right amount of humidity and air circulation.

PERENNIALS

A second blooming. Most perennial flowers naturally flower for a period of several weeks once every year. Some, however, will produce a second flush of flowers if they are cut back after the first period of bloom. Plants that respond to this treatment include Siberian iris, snowdrop anemone, dwarf baby's breath, lythrum, cranesbill, and 'Miss Lingard' phlox.

Filling in the gaps. The foliage of some perennials—notably poppies, bluebells, and bleeding hearts—withers after the plants finish blooming. To ensure that gaps don't open up in the beds, set such fast faders among expansive, more persistent plants such as hostas, lamb's ears, or iberises.

When to plant. Where winters are cold and wet, or in gardens with heavy, clayey soil, plant perennials in the spring, after the soil warms. Where winters are mild or soils are sandy and light, plant in the fall.

Striking foliage. Many perennials contribute more with their foliage than their flowers. Hostas, for example, produce broad and colorful leaves that may be green, blue, or golden, and striped or splashed with cream or white; the flowers are relatively insignificant. Other outstanding foliage plants include the gold-spotted leopard plant (*Ligularia tussilaginea* 'Aureomaculata), and the fuzzy-leaved silver sage *(Salvia argentea)*.

Highlights of texture. Perennial foliage also contributes textures. Spiny-leaved bear's-breech *(Acanthus spinosus)* and the plump cushions of 'Silver Mound' wormwood *(Artemisia schmidtiana)* each give a planting a different feel.

ANNUALS

Hardy annuals tolerate cold weather and even some frost. Examples: annual baby's-breath, annual phlox, clarkia, common sunflower, cornflower, crown daisy, godetia, golden coreopsis, larkspur, pansy, sweet alyssum, and toadflax. Sow seed directly into beds whenever the soil can be worked—fall in mild climates, early spring in cooler regions.

Half-hardy annuals tolerate cool temperatures but only very light frosts. Sow seed indoors and transplant out after weather moderates. Butter daisy, California poppy, cleome, dusty miller, four o'clock, gerbera, Iceland poppy, kochia, lantana, morning glory, nierembergia, rainbow pink—all these are half-hardy.

Tender annuals, plants that die after the first hard frost, include ageratum, cockscomb, coleus, cosmos, garden verbena, globe amaranth, impatiens, lobelia, marigold, moss rose, nicotiana, petunia, scarlet sage, wax begonia, zinnia. Sow only in warm soil. In Northern climates sow indoors and plant out only after all danger of frost has passed.

Fertilizing for flowers. Don't fertilize annual flowers with manure. The nitrogen-rich animal dung encourages rampant leaf growth at the expense of flower production. Instead, feed with compost or a commercial fertilizer formulated with a relatively low nitrogen content.

Deadheading flowers. To keep annuals blooming all summer long, snip off aging flowers before they produce seeds. This encourages plants to put their energy into new growth rather than seed production and helps make them stronger.

BULBS

Planting bulbs. A well-drained site is essential for most bulbs; if your soil is a heavy silt or clayey, dig plenty of coarse sand and compost into the bed before planting. To keep chipmunks, squirrels, and mice from feeding on bulbs, bury a piece of large-holed wire mesh over plantings. Or sprinkle moth crystals over freshly planted bulbs.

Planting depths. In general, a bulb should be planted at a depth at least twice its height. Exceptions to this rule include oriental and Asiatic lilies whose bulbs should be planted at 3 to 4 times their depth, and the Madonna lily which should be planted with the top of the bulb just below the soil surface.

Effects to achieve. For the best visual effect, plant bulbs in groups, not singly or in rows. For a naturalistic effect, toss bulbs onto the ground and plant them wherever they fall.

Feed spring bulbs during their growing season by irrigating them with a water-soluble fertilizer. High potassium fertilizers formulated for tomatoes are especially good.

Weed by hand in beds planted with bulbs—pointed tools can easily injure shallowly planted bulbs or bulb roots.

Store tender bulbs such as dahlias, cannas, tuberous begonias, and caladiums indoors through the winter in cold-weather regions. Keep the stored bulbs from shrivelling by packing them in slightly moistened sand or sawdust; arrange the bulbs so that no two touch each other.

Buying Trees & Shrubs

You can use the suggestions in the checklist below when you buy either trees or shrubs.

❑ Check for leaves that are torn or brown along the margin. Such leaves indicate that the plant was exposed to excessive wind during shipment.

❑ Look for yellowed leaves. These usually indicate that the plant was left unwatered too long or exposed to excessive sun or heat. In either case, the result is damaged roots that cannot support the foliage.

❑ Check the trunk. Bruises or scars in the bark are evidence of rough handling and may conceal serious injury to the growing tissue underneath.

❑ Check to make sure there are no splits in the crotches where major branches emerge from the trunk.

❑ Check for stubs of cut-back branches. This is a sign of unskilled pruning and suggests that the tree or shrub hasn't received good care. It may also indicate that mistreatment has caused the plant to die back.

❑ When shopping for conifers, run a hand over the foliage—if it feels dry, that's an indication that the plant's root ball has been allowed to dry out at some point, even if it is moist at the time of inspection. Conifers rarely recover from that kind of stress.

❑ Buy younger, smaller plants. Larger specimens suffer far more trauma from transplanting and are slower to resume normal growth. Often a small tree will shoot up to overtake the larger specimen within a few years.

PRUNING

The best time of year to prune most trees and shrubs is at the end of their dormant period, at the beginning of their new season of growth. An exception to this rule is flowering shrubs, whose pruning should be timed to enhance the quality of their bloom. Prune shrubs that bloom in spring—forsythias and rhododendrons, for example—immediately after they flower. Shrubs that flower later in the summer or fall and that bloom on the new growth (such as hybrid tea roses) should be pruned in early spring, just as the new growth begins to emerge.

How to make the cut. Years ago, gardening wisdom on removing tree limbs dictated that the final cut should be flush with the trunk; the goal was to achieve a flat profile. Recent research, however, indicates that healing is faster and healthier when limbs are cut off just outside the collar—the thickened ridge of wood and bark that surrounds the base of the limb.

Pruning wounds heal best if left untreated. So-called pruning paints and wound dressings actually slow the healing process and promote decay.

The right tool. For removing small branches, those 1/2 in/1.3 cm thick or less, the best tool is a pair of bypass pruning shears. These have curved-edge blades that cut with a scissorlike action. Blade-and-anvil shears cut by pressing the branch between a flat-edged blade and a metal anvil; these crush as they cut, causing unnecessary injury to the plant.

When pruning diseased branches from a tree or shrub, as with roses infected with black spot or apple trees infected with fire blight, your pruning tools can spread the disease from plant to plant. To avoid this, disinfect the tools between cuts by dipping the blades of the tool in a solution of 1 part chlorine bleach or alcohol to 9 parts water.

Maintain your shears so that they will be useful for many years. Not only do well-maintained tools last longer, they are easier to use and make a cleaner cut. To care for your shears, lubricate the pivot area regularly with a light machine oil or petroleum jelly. Sharpen the blade regularly with a fine file or stone and replace the blade when it becomes worn. If the blades become stained with sap, clean them with light oil and steel wool.

Trimming a hedge. Don't overprune with a hedge trimmer. It is better to trim lightly and then go over the hedge a second time only if it is necessary.

Safety measures. Prevent accidents when using a power trimmer. Wear clothing that fits snugly; a loose shirt can get caught in the blade. When lowering the trimmer to your side, be careful not to hit your leg or catch your clothing.

Vegetables

A sunny spot. When planting a vegetable garden, put it in the sunniest spot available. Most vegetables require at least 6 hours of sunlight a day.

Shade lovers. Some greens flourish in conditions of partial shade. Among them are several old favorites: arugula, cabbage, chicory, collards, endive, escarole, kale, lettuce, mustard greens, perilla, radicchio, spinach, Swiss chard, and turnips.

Row by row. In temperate climates run rows from east to west so that all the plants receive maximum sunshine. In hot, arid climates run rows from north to south to let each plant be shaded by its neighbors as the sun moves across the sky.

How wide is your garden? Stepping on soil within the beds compacts the soil, depriving roots of air and water. To prevent this make beds no more than 4 ft/1.2 m wide so that all planting and tending may be done while standing outside the bed and reaching in.

Tall order. Plant taller crops, such as corn and pole beans, at the north end of the garden, so they won't shade their neighbors.

Harvesting lettuce. If you water leafy greens in the evening and then pick them the next morning, they'll be crisp and full of flavor. For an extended harvest, plant leaf lettuces which may be picked leaf by leaf over a period of weeks. When harvesting Swiss chard, use your hands and break off leaves at the base. Don't use a knife; it could injure the inner stems and prevent further growth.

Thirsty crops. Drought slows vegetable growth, harms harvest quality and flavor, and may even abort fruit production. Be sure to give all vegetables at least 1 in/2.5 cm of water per week during rainless weather. Adequate moisture is especially important for leafy crops as they approach harvest size, for root crops as the roots start to expand, and for fruiting vegetables as they set flowers.

Strategies for a small garden. Reap maximum harvests from small gardens by planting climbing crops, such as pole beans, cucumbers, or squash, which can be trained up trellises and so occupy little bed space. Or grow vegetables in tubs, planting dwarf varieties, specially bred for container cultivation—tomatoes, cabbages, cucumbers, and more.

A path for a large garden. Run a 3-ft/90-cm-wide path of bricks, concrete pavers, or wooden planks down the center of the garden to provide access for a cart or wheelbarrow.

Rotating crops. Confuse the pests and diseases that overwinter in the soil by changing the location of each crop annually. Also, use one crop to prepare the soil for the next. Grow heavy feeders (lettuce and corn, for instance) in freshly manured soil; by drawing excess nutrients from the soil, they leave the plot in ideal condition for beets, onions, carrots, turnips and other root crops. Follow these with cabbage or its relatives—broccoli, Brussels sprouts, collards, and kale.

For many gardeners, browsing through mail order catalogs of plants and tools is a joy in itself. And shopping by catalog offers access to a vast selection of plants and tools. When it comes to buying plant material and tools through the mail, however, you have to plan to make sure that your order arrives when you want it to. Shopping by mail requires patience: you can't buy on a whim the way you can at a local garden center or nursery. Depending on your needs, you may find that a combination of local resources and catalogs serve you best.

Here are the names, addresses, and telephone numbers of some mail-order suppliers, a small sampling of those available to gardeners. You'll find room room to add your own discoveries on the pages that follow.

GENERAL NURSERY STOCK

W. Atlee Burpee Company
300 Park Avenue
Warminster, PA 18974
(215) 674-4900, (800) 888-1447

Emphasis on flower and vegetable seeds; perennials, trees, shrubs, tools and supplies as well

R. H. Shumway Seedsman
571 Whaley Pond Road
Graniteville, SC 29829
(803) 663-9771

Seeds, plants, and supplies

Wayside Gardens
PO Box 1
Hodges, SC 29695
(800) 845-1124

Selection of trees, shrubs, perennials, and roses

BULBS

Jacques Amand, Bulb Specialists
P.O. Box 59001
Potomac, MD 20859
(301) 762-6601, (800) 452-5414

Spring and summer blooming bulbs, many unusual species and cultivars

B & D Lilies
330 P Street
Port Townshend, WA 98368
(360) 385-1738

Hybrid and species lilies

The Daffodil Mart
7463 Heath Trail
Gloucester, VA 23061
(804) 693-3966

More than 1,000 species and cultivars of spring and summer bulbs with special emphasis on narcissus

FRUITS

Bay Laurel Nursery
2500 El Camino Real
Altascadero, CA 93422
(805) 466-3406

Fruit and nut trees, berries, wine grapes, and table grapes

Exotica Rare Fruit Nursery
P.O. Box 160
2508-B East Vista Way
Vista, CA 92085
(619) 724-9393
(619) 724-7724 (fax)

Tropical fruits, flowering trees & nuts

Southmeadow Fruit Gardens
15310 Red Arrow Highway
Baroda, MI 49101
(616) 422-2411

Fruit trees, including many antique varieties; wild berries and fruits to attract wildlife

NATIVE PLANTS & WILD FLOWERS

Gardens of the Blue Ridge
PO Box 10
9056 Pittman Gap Road
North Pineola, NC 28662
(704) 733-2417

Eastern woodland and meadow wildflowers, ferns, trees and shrubs

Prairie Nursery
P.O. Box 306
Westfield, WI 53964
(608) 296-3679

Prairie grasses and flowers, as plants or custom-mixed seed blends

Plants of the Southwest
Route 6, Box 11A, Agua Fria
Santa Fe, NM 87501
(505) 438-8888

Drought-proof trees, shrubs, flowers, and grasses

PERENNIAL FLOWERS

Andre Viette Farm & Nursery
Route 1, Box 16
State Route 608
Fisherville, VA 22939
(540) 942-2118

Perennials and ornamental grasses

Kurt Bluemel, Inc.
10603 Cleveland Avenue
Baldwin, MD 21013
(410) 557-7229

Ornamental grasses, perennials, bamboos, ferns and water plants

Klehm Nursery
4210 North Duncan Road
Champaign, IL 61821
(217) 359-2888

Hostas, daylilies, peonies, and many other perennial flowers and grasses

Trees, shrubs, and roses

Carroll Gardens
P.O. Box 310
444 E. Main Street
Westminster, MD 21158
(410) 848-5422, (800) 638-6334

Trees, shrubs, roses, and vines;
also perennials and bulbs

Heronswood Nursery
7530 288th N.E. Street
Kingston, WA 98346
(360) 297-4172

Choice and rare ornamental trees
and shrubs

Hortico, Inc.
723 Robson Road, RR1
Waterdown, ON
Canada
LOR 2H1
(905) 839-2111

Roses; perennials, trees, and shrubs

Vegetables and herbs

The Cook's Garden
P.O. Box 535
Moffits Bridge
Londonderry, VT 05148
(802) 824-3400
(802) 824-3027 (fax)

Gourmet and reliable vegetables

Nichol's Garden Nursery, Inc.
1190 N. Pacific Highway
Albany, OR 97321
(541) 928-9280

Herbs and herbal supplies; also
vegetable and flower seeds

Ronniger's Seed Potatoes
Star Route, Road 73
Moyie Springs, ID 83845
No telephone orders

Potatoes; garlics, onions, shallots

Territorial Seed Company
P.O. Box 157
Cottage Grove, OR 97424
(541) 942-9547

Vegetable cultivars adapted to the Northwest

Tomato Growers Supply Company
P.O. Box 2237
Fort Myers, FL 33902
(941) 768-1119

Tomatoes and peppers

Tools and supplies

A.M. Leonard, Inc.
P.O. Box 816
241 Fox Drive
Piqua, OH 45356
(513) 773-2694

Tools of every kind

PERSONAL DIRECTORY

Name

Address

Telephone number

Specialty

Name

Address

Telephone number

Specialty

Name

Address

Telephone number

Specialty

Name

Address

Telephone number

Specialty

PERSONAL DIRECTORY

Name

Address

Telephone number

Specialty

Name

Address

Telephone number

Specialty

Name

Address

Telephone number

Specialty

Name

Address

Telephone number

Specialty

Name

Address

Telephone number

Specialty

Name

Address

Telephone number

Specialty

Name

Address

Telephone number

Specialty

Name

Address

Telephone number

Specialty